DISCOVER
Your Career

Careers If You Like

Problem-Solving

Leanne Currie-McGhee

ReferencePoint Press

San Diego, CA

ReferencePoint Press®

Printed in the United States

For more information, contact:
ReferencePoint Press, Inc.
PO Box 27779
San Diego, CA 92198
www.ReferencePointPress.com

LIBRARY OF CONGRESS CATALOGING-IN-PUBLICATION DATA

Names: Currie-McGhee, Leanne, 1971- author
Title: Careers if you like problem-solving / Leanne Currie-McGhee.
Description: San Diego, CA : ReferencePoint Press, 2025. | Series: Discover your career | Includes bibliographical references and index.
Identifiers: LCCN 2025025002 (print) | LCCN 2025025003 (ebook) | ISBN 9781678212186 library binding | ISBN 9781678212193 ebook
Subjects: LCSH: Occupations--Juvenile literature | Problem-solving--Juvenile literature
Classification: LCC HF5381.2 .C872 2025 (print) | LCC HF5381.2 (ebook)
LC record available at https://lccn.loc.gov/2025025002
LC ebook record available at https://lccn.loc.gov/2025025003

Contents

Introduction: A Way of Thinking

Do you love strategizing how to build defenses in *Minecraft* to protect your base from creepers? Or maybe you get so caught up in a tricky math word problem that you lose track of time, completely focused until you find the solution. Perhaps you even enjoy reorganizing your closet just to make everything fit perfectly. If any of these sound like you, chances are you enjoy solving problems, big or small. And that skill could lead you toward a fulfilling career.

This has been the case for Akanksha Chapra, who loved problem-solving activities as a child. "I was fascinated by jigsaw puzzles, spending hours piecing together intricate designs," she writes. "This love for deciphering complex patterns and finding hidden solutions naturally led me to the field of data analytics."[1] After graduating with a computer science degree and then working as a software engineer for several years, she returned to school to focus on data analysis. In 2025 she graduated from Northeastern University in Massachusetts with a master's degree in informatics with a concentration in analytics. Her early interest led her to a career focused on using critical thinking and technology to develop solutions to different business challenges, from improving customer experiences to identifying trends that guide company decisions.

For Chapra, problem-solving is more than just a skill—it is a way of thinking. In today's world, where careers constantly change as technology evolves, someone who can think critically is more valuable than ever. It is a transferable skill that can be used in all types of industries.

Areas in Need

Although the ability to solve problems is a valuable skill in most any field, in some career fields problem-solving is central to the work. This is especially true as technology evolves and businesses are flooded with vast amounts of data. Making sense of this information requires analytical minds—people who can interpret data trends, identify patterns, and make data-driven decisions. People working as data scientists, business intelligence analysts, data engineers, and machine learning engineers are among those who turn raw data into meaningful insights. Their problem-solving skills help businesses make smart decisions, predict outcomes, and improve operations.

Analytical thinkers are also sought out in all areas of engineering. Whether it is a civil engineer figuring out how to design a building that can withstand hurricanes, a mechanical engineer troubleshooting a factory's production system, or an environmental engineer determining how to clean up an oil spill, problem-solving is at the heart of the work. Engineers innovate to make life more efficient, safe, and sustainable for people.

Problem solvers can also find careers in areas that do not require a four-year college degree. Skilled trade workers like electricians, plumbers, and automotive technicians face puzzles daily, whether it is solving a power outage or diagnosing the cause of failing brakes. Other types of jobs that do not require college degrees are information technology support specialists and network technicians, who unravel technology problems and keep entire businesses running.

Transforming Challenge to Solution

A problem-solving mindset enables teens to deal with life's challenges and equips them for future career opportunities. Learning to find creative solutions to challenges can develop critical thinking abilities that open a teen's future up to a variety of careers. Amara Nwuneli, a seventeen-year-old from Nigeria, faced a very big problem in 2020, after she and her family and their neighbors were displaced by a devastating flood. The hardships they encountered in the aftermath of the flood led Nwuneli to think about the role of climate change in contributing to their predicament.

Her response was to establish a nonprofit organization called Preserve Our Roots. The organization's focus is on making Nwuneli's neighborhood greener, more resilient to flooding, and more livable for the residents. One project involved turning a waste site into a playground. The slides and a climbing wall were made from recycled materials. As part of that project, the group also planted over three hundred flood-resistant trees around the park. Reflecting on her journey, Nwuneli said, "I'm not satisfied. I feel like every community needs this."[2] Her work earned her the 2025 Earth Prize and a $12,500 award from the Earth Foundation, which she plans to use to build three additional eco-friendly parks in other parts of Nigeria. Nwuneli used her problem-solving skills to create something good out of a bad situation. In the process, she created her own organization and took steps toward a lifelong career.

What Nwuneli has discovered is that no matter a person's background or career goals, the ability to think through problems, ask questions, and seek better solutions is a skill that can take them far. As a teen, being open to exploring new possibilities and taking chances can be the first step toward a meaningful future.

Forensic Scientist

What Does a Forensic Scientist Do?

Forensic scientists solve the puzzles of real-life mysteries. They are part of teams—often working with law enforcement agencies—that unravel crimes by analyzing physical evidence and offering scientific insights into what happened. No matter the crime, there are clues: blood, fingerprints, fibers, text messages, and online searches. "It's impossible, frankly, to eradicate every single jot of evidence in a crime scene. So, the mistakes that [criminals] make—apart from not really fully understanding the potential of forensic science—is they forget that they're leaving traces of themselves on every surface that they touch, on every path that they take,"[3] explains Jo Millington, a forensic scientist who specializes in analyzing blood patterns and has worked on high-profile court cases in the United Kingdom.

Forensic scientists like Millington are trained to interpret these clues and reconstruct the events of the crime. They may work onsite to find and collect clues, or

At a Glance

Number of Jobs
Approximately twenty-seven hundred openings per year*

Pay
Average salary of $79,408 annually in 2025

Educational Requirements
Bachelor's degree in forensic science, chemistry, biology, or a related scientific field

Personal Qualities
Detail-oriented, curious, analytical

Working Conditions
Labs, crime scenes, and medical examiners' offices

Future Job Outlook
Growth of 14 percent through 2033*

* Numbers are for the related career of forensic science technicians

they may spend much of their time in laboratories testing and studying the evidence.

Unlike television crime shows, which often depict one dynamic forensic scientist doing every test under the sun with immediate and definitive results, real-world forensic science is slow and precise. And most of the professionals in this field work in different specialties, from deoxyribonucleic acid (DNA) analysis and toxicology to digital forensics and ballistics. The goal of forensic science is to connect the dots, build timelines, and determine how the evidence fits into a larger story. For example, a forensic scientist who specializes in DNA may study skin cells to match genetic material to a suspect in a murder case. In another case, a forensic scientist might determine whether a victim died from alcohol or drug poisoning by analyzing blood alcohol concentration and other bodily fluids for toxicity levels. Every piece of information they uncover helps determine the details and actions of the crime. Forensic scientists are part of a team that works to figure out who committed the crime, what happened, and—sometimes—who the victims were.

A Typical Workday

How a forensic scientist's workday unfolds depends on their role and specialty. Some spend most of their time in laboratories, examining DNA, bodily fluids, and fingerprints. Others specialize in digital forensics, scanning hard drives for deleted files. Some may focus on firearms analysis, studying bullets to determine what weapon was used. Others might work directly at crime scenes to collect evidence firsthand. Many combine several of these responsibilities.

The day may begin with reviewing a case file, then running tests in the lab and studying the results. Afterward, the scientist may write detailed reports explaining the findings and what they mean. George Schiro became interested in police work and forensic science as a child. Today, he works as a DNA technical leader/

Combining Science and Mysteries

"I didn't realize I wanted to be a forensic scientist until I was at LSU [Louisiana State University]. I was majoring in microbiology with a pre-med option when I decided that I didn't want to go to medical school. My best friend suggested that I look into a crime lab career. That's when it hit me like a bolt of lightning. That's exactly the career I wanted. Ever since I was a young boy growing up in New Orleans, I was interested in police work, mysteries, and science. This type of career seemed to be a perfect mix of my interests."

—George Schiro, forensic scientist, Scales Biological Laboratory

Quoted in Erin Kent, "Interview with George Schiro, Forensic Scientist, Scales Biological Laboratory," eLearners. www.elearners.com.

forensic scientist in Missouri. His day typically includes DNA testing of specimens related to human identity, paternity, and crime scenes. He also performs laboratory analysis of other evidence such as fingerprints, footprints, and bloodstain patterns.

As a lead scientist, Schiro oversees all DNA operations in the lab. "As DNA technical leader, I am responsible for the lab's DNA operations and its quality assurance. I have administrative duties as well, such as payroll, invoicing, drafting reports, paperwork, and carrying out other quality assurance activities,"[4] Schiro explains. Report writing can occupy large chunks of a day. Reports explain test results and conclusions, which might be needed for use by attorneys in court proceedings. At times, forensic scientists are asked to testify in court as expert witnesses. In this role, forensic scientists use their experience, skills, and knowledge to assist the court in understanding technical scientific issues such as what blood splatter patterns show or the likelihood that DNA from a crime belongs to the defendant. As Schiro has found, no two days are the same. The work of a forensic scientist blends science, analysis, and communication to help determine what happened in a crime.

A forensic scientist tests a hammer for traces of blood and DNA. These professionals help members of law enforcement unravel crimes by analyzing and evaluating physical evidence.

Education and Training

High school students who have an interest in forensic science can prepare for this field by taking biology, chemistry, and other science courses. The path to becoming a forensic scientist usually begins with a bachelor's degree in forensic science, chemistry, biology, or a related scientific field. Programs in forensics include coursework in toxicology, molecular biology, criminal justice, genetics, and physics.

Coursework for a forensic science degree typically includes traditional classroom learning as well as hands-on training. Forensic science students at George Washington University in Washington, DC, practice proper evidence collection methods in houses that have been built to simulate crime scenes. They also learn in outdoor "body farms," which are outdoor areas where donated bodies have been placed, and study how real human remains decompose over time. These practical experiences develop observational skills and teach students how to document evidence that will hold up in court.

Those who seek higher positions, such as managing or directing a forensic unit, often pursue higher degrees to further their education and boost their chances of advancement. Some forensic scientists also pursue professional certifications that demonstrate expertise in a given area. For instance, some of these professionals become certified criminalists, which recognizes individuals who have demonstrated proficiency in the field of criminology.

Skills and Personality

This career is ideal for individuals who are methodical, curious, and comfortable working both independently and as part of a team. Attention to detail is essential; forensic scientists must be able to observe details at crime scenes, detect patterns and spot inconsistencies in evidence, and think critically when analyzing the information and evidence.

Problem-solving lies at the heart of the job. Whether they are trying to match a fingerprint or determine a timeline of events, forensic scientists must be logical thinkers who can follow the information they obtain and interpret it. Communication skills are also vital. Scientists must explain their findings to people with little or no scientific background, including police officers, lawyers, or jury members. Their reports must be clear, concise, and accurate enough to hold up in court.

Workplace Settings

Work settings vary by specialization. Those focused on lab work usually operate in clean, controlled environments. Crime scene investigators may travel, work outdoors, and face high-stress or physically difficult conditions. Location also affects the job. In larger cities with higher crime rates, forensic departments tend to be bigger, and professionals may focus on one specialty, like blood spatter or DNA. In smaller towns, forensic scientists may handle evidence collection at crime scenes and analysis in the lab.

Impactful Career

"There is no one single day that is exactly the same as the other one. It's very diverse . . . it's why I love it, because you feel that you contribute to a discipline that is being shaped. You try to use your scientific knowledge to address real life problems—how your knowledge can be used to solve crime and cases, disrupt, and prevent some cases, so you've got this big, potential societal impact which I think is very motivating."

—Claude Roux, director of Centre for Forensic Science, University of Technology Sydney

—Quoted in Tanna Nankivell, "How to Become a Forensic Scientist—Experiences of a Distinguished Professor of Forensic Science at UTS," Art of Smart, 2024. https://artofsmart.com.au.

The job can involve long hours, especially in urgent or high-profile cases. The work can also be emotionally taxing, as scientists may encounter disturbing materials such as autopsy photos or evidence from violent crimes. Forensic scientists must find healthy ways to manage the emotional demands of the job. While the workload can vary, the work always requires intense focus and a strong commitment to accuracy—a single mistake in evidence interpretation can have serious consequences.

Employers and Pay

Most forensic scientists work for local or state government crime labs, though some are employed by federal agencies such as the Federal Bureau of Investigation, Drug Enforcement Administration, or US Department of Homeland Security. Others work in medical examiners' offices or hospitals or serve as consultants for private investigative firms. They may also find work with private labs, law firms, research institutions, or universities.

As of April 2025, according to the online job search platform ZipRecruiter, forensic scientists in the United States earned an average annual salary of $79,408, with reported salaries ranging from around $36,500 to $137,500. Salaries can vary based on factors such as experience, education, specialization, location, and employer.

What Is the Future Outlook for Forensic Scientists?

For teens considering a career in forensic science, the future looks promising. According to the Bureau of Labor Statistics (BLS), employment for forensic science technicians is projected to grow 14 percent through 2033, much faster than the average for all occupations. Forensic science technicians have similar roles as forensic scientists, and in some places their titles are used interchangeably. However, technicians usually perform more hands-on technical work, such as collecting and processing evidence, while forensic scientists often have more advanced roles, which may include interpreting results. Because specific statistics for forensic scientists alone are harder to find, industry trends regarding technicians suggest their job growth is similar, since many technicians move into scientist roles.

On average, about twenty-seven hundred job openings are expected each year for forensic science technicians, according to the BLS, driven by retirements, job changes, and growing demand. The growth in this field is fueled by increasing reliance on forensic evidence in investigations and significant advances in areas like DNA technology, digital forensics, and lab automation.

As crime solving becomes more science driven, the need for trained forensic professionals is only expected to rise. If analyzing blood spatter to understand how a crime occurred, interpreting DNA to help catch a suspect, or presenting evidence in court sounds intriguing, a career in forensic science offers exciting opportunities to make a real-world impact.

Find Out More

American Academy of Forensic Sciences

www.aafs.org

This professional organization offers information on careers in forensic science, including specialty areas like toxicology, anthropology, and digital forensics. Its website includes educational resources, student membership opportunities, and details about college programs.

American Board of Criminalistics

www.criminalistics.com

This board certifies forensic scientists in areas like DNA, trace evidence, and crime scene investigation. Its website outlines certification requirements, study materials, and resources for those pursuing a career in forensic science.

International Association for Identification

www.theiai.org

This association supports professionals in forensic identification fields such as fingerprints, footwear, DNA, and facial recognition. It offers training opportunities, conferences, certification programs, and job listings for current and aspiring forensic scientists.

Environmental Engineer

What Does an Environmental Engineer Do?

Imagine a tanker truck overturns on a busy highway, spilling oil onto the surrounding area. Within hours, environmental engineers would be among the professionals called to the scene. They would help determine and implement containment measures, including the use of specialized materials to absorb the hazardous substance. They would decide how to reduce immediate dangers and plan for long-term environmental recovery.

At a Glance

Number of Jobs
Approximately 41,300 jobs in 2023

Pay
Average salary of $104,170 in 2024

Educational Requirements
Bachelor's degree in environmental engineering or a related field

Personal Qualities
Creative, logical, detail-oriented

Working Conditions
Offices, laboratories, industrial sites, and outdoor fieldwork

Future Job Outlook
Growth of 7 percent through 2033

Environmental engineers work to protect the world and its people from pollution and other harmful practices that threaten the environment. They apply technology and science to promote responsible use and management of natural resources to meet the needs of today without harming the ability of future generations to meet their needs. They focus on critical issues such as pollution control, water quality, and sustainable infrastructure design. Their work often requires balancing environmental protection and economic development.

A key part of their job involves analyzing the environmental impact of projects and finding ways to minimize any negative effects. For example, a team of environmental engineers might assess the impact of a planned mining project on people, water, and wildlife. They would then propose safer alternatives, like reducing resource use, shrinking the work zone, and applying the latest technology to cut down on pollution. Through their work, they help preserve the planet and shape a more sustainable future.

A Typical Workday

A typical workday for an environmental engineer depends on their area of focus and where they work, but the main goal is always the same. They look for ways to protect the environment. Kayla Fairbairn is an environmental engineer with an engineering consulting company in New Zealand. Her clients are businesses that need to make sure they are meeting national and local environmental regulations. She monitors air and water quality near businesses to prevent pollution. Each day, she receives air contaminant data from sites across New Zealand. She reviews this information to look for patterns of rising pollutants such as nitrogen dioxide (NO_2). Then she advises her clients on how they can reduce their emissions. "We typically draw up the data in different types of graphics to clearly show and explain how air contaminants are going to affect nearby residents. If there were high NO_2 concentrations in a wide radius around the industrial emitter, that can mean residents nearby are really negatively affected,"[5] Fairbairn explains. Fairbairn is proud to be part of making a cleaner and greener New Zealand through her work.

While Fairbairn mainly works in an office, other environmental engineers split their time between the field and the office. That is the case for Hannah Olonovich, an environmental manager for a construction company that has projects nationwide. She gained experience as an environmental engineer before obtaining a management position in the field. She ensures that construction projects follow environmental rules for air, water, waste, and soil. But

Lasting Impact

"[Being an environmental engineer] allows you the opportunity to work outdoors or indoors, with field work, to really understand what's happening in our environment, and in our water, and in our air. And it gives you the opportunity to have a long-lasting impact on the world. Everyone has a right to clean water, breathable air, a place to properly dispose of their waste that doesn't affect our environment and having a well conserved clean and healthy environment."

—Imari Walker, doctoral student at Duke University studying environmental engineering

Imari Walker, *Why You Should Major in Environmental Engineering?*, YouTube, 2021. www.youtube.com/watch?v=udUbkcCda0s.

her work is not just about meeting regulations—it is also about finding ways to reduce the company's environmental impact and protect public health.

Olonovich visits jobsites to monitor equipment like rock crushers, testing for air particles that could be harmful if not properly controlled. If the emissions are too high, she documents the issue, investigates what is causing the increase (such as a clogged filter or overloaded machine), and works with her team to fix it.

After heavy rainfall, she might also collect stormwater samples to make sure runoff from construction sites is not carrying pollution into nearby rivers or streams. Back at the office, she stays on top of environmental permits and files paperwork to make sure her company complies with local, state, and federal requirements. A big part of her job is solving problems as they come up on-site. For example, her team once considered relocating a rock crusher to reduce its impact on the public and meet local environmental regulations. However, moving it would have required new permits, and applying for those permits would have been very costly. "Thoroughly knowing how the regulatory process works, I was able to find a situation that met all the requirements—without a relocation, and ultimately saved the company $25K,"[6] Olonovich recalls.

Education and Training

If teens are contemplating an environmental engineering path, the best preparation is to take honors and advanced placement classes in science courses such as chemistry and environmental science and mathematics courses such as calculus. Joining environmental clubs or volunteering with organizations can help teens explore their interest in environmental issues.

Following high school, the path to becoming an environmental engineer typically includes a bachelor's degree in environmental engineering or a related field such as environmental science or civil, chemical, or mechanical engineering. These programs often include coursework in subjects like calculus, chemistry, biology, geology, and environmental science.

Doing an internship while in college is a good way to get real-world experience and find out whether the work truly suits your interests. "Gaining experience is vital—for you to figure out your . . . career path but to also have a leg-up when you're applying for jobs,"[7] says Olonovich.

Those who want to do research or achieve higher-level management positions typically obtain a master's degree or PhD. Additionally, obtaining a Professional Engineer license is crucial for those who are in careers in which they sign off on plans for projects and submit plans to regulatory bodies. Requirements for licensure vary by state but typically include a combination of education, work experience, and a passing score on relevant exams.

Skills and Personality

Environmental engineering is well suited for analytical, detail-oriented, and collaborative individuals. Strong problem-solving skills are essential, since engineers often tackle complex issues

An environmental engineer tests a river's water quality. Monitoring pollutant levels from construction, mining, agriculture, and other human activities is one of the jobs of an environmental engineer.

like pollution control, waste management, and resource conservation. They must be able to identify potential problems and find ways to prevent them. Additionally, environmental engineers must be dedicated to continually learning in their field to keep up with technological advances and changing regulations.

Collaboration is a key component of the job. Engineers frequently work in teams, coordinating with other engineers, scientists, industry representatives, urban planners, and government officials. "The most important trait to work through tough situations is collaboration! I wouldn't have been able to succeed if I didn't have a team that I could consistently run ideas by and hear educated feedback,"[8] explains Olonovich. Good communication skills are vital for engaging in this type of collaboration, as well as for presenting findings, writing reports, and explaining technical information to laypeople.

Workplace Settings

Environmental engineers work in diverse settings, including offices, laboratories, and field sites. They may be employed by government agencies, private consulting firms, or corporations. Their work often

Going Green

"My signature project here in the MTA [Metropolitan Transit Authority] is the Mother Clara Hale bus depot. The building includes a green roof, which is a vegetative roof which absorbs rainwater, absorbs carbon dioxide, adds an extra layer of insulation to the roof and also absorbs floating particles in the atmosphere. There's also a rooftop rainwater collection system which drains into a 50,000 gallon tank and we use that rainwater to wash the buses."

—Tom Abdallah, vice president of design services and chief environmental engineer at Metropolitan Transportation Authority

Quoted in Metropolitan Transit Authority, *What Does a Chief Environmental Engineer Do?*, YouTube, 2023, www.youtube.com/watch?v=7Wzq3ai3L2U.

involves desk-based tasks, like data analysis and report writing, and on-site activities, such as inspecting facilities or collecting environmental samples. For instance, an environmental engineer might split time between lab work and field inspections at construction sites. In urban areas, engineers might focus on issues like air quality and waste management, while in rural settings, they may address concerns related to agriculture or natural resource conservation.

Environmental engineers often work a typical workweek with weekends off and regular hours. However, they may work weekends and nights if they are assigned to a project with a deadline or there is an emergency like an oil spill. The job requires flexibility, attention to detail, and a commitment to protecting public health and the environment.

Employers and Pay

As of May 2024, environmental engineers in the United States earned an average annual salary of $104,170 according to the Bureau of Labor Statistics (BLS). However, actual salaries can vary depending on several factors, including experience, level of education, specific areas of specialization, and location. Environmental engineers have strong earning potential, especially as they gain experience or pursue leadership roles in their fields.

Environmental engineers are employed across a wide range of industries. Many work for government agencies, where they contribute to public infrastructure projects, help develop environmental policies, and ensure compliance with environmental regulations. Others are employed by private consulting firms, where they provide expert guidance to businesses on environmental impact assessments and sustainable practices. Large corporations also hire environmental engineers to help ensure their operations comply with environmental standards and to lead efforts to reduce their ecological footprint. Additionally, nonprofit organizations offer opportunities for environmental engineers to engage in conservation efforts, promote public education, and advocate for environmental protection.

What Is the Future Outlook for Environmental Engineers?

The demand for environmental engineers continues to grow as society places increasing importance on sustainability and addressing the impacts of climate change. This growth presents promising career opportunities for those passionate about using their skills to protect the environment and improve public health. According to the BLS, employment in this field is projected to grow 7 percent through 2033, faster than the average for all occupations.

The BLS also indicates that approximately three thousand job openings for environmental engineers are expected each year over the next decade, resulting from the need to replace retiring workers and increasing focus on environmental concerns. Advancements in technology, such as renewable energy systems and pollution control methods, are also creating new opportunities in the field. Randy Ly, a water resource control engineer for the California State Water Resources Control Board, says, "Climate change is an undeniable reality. . . . Environmental engineers are at the forefront of developing and implementing strategies to mitigate these effects. For example, they design systems to manage stormwater runoff in urban areas to prevent flooding, which is a problem that is becoming more common with changing weather patterns."[9] For teens interested in working on these types of issues, a career in environmental engineering offers the chance to contribute to meaningful projects that protect natural resources and promote public health.

Find Out More

American Academy of Environmental Engineers & Scientists
www.aaees.org
This organization certifies environmental engineers and scientists who have demonstrated expertise in the field. Its website features student resources, scholarship opportunities, and guidance on career development in the field. The site also offers information on board certification, mentoring possibilities, and annual awards that recognize outstanding contributions to the profession.

National Association of Environmental Professionals (NAEP)
www.naep.org
NAEP supports environmental professionals, including those in engineering, policy, and planning. Its website provides access to career webinars, a job board, student memberships, and information about its annual conference. The site also provides information for students and recent graduates looking to enter the environmental field.

Society of Women Engineers (SWE)
https://swe.org
The SWE advocates for women in engineering and technology fields, including environmental engineering. Its site offers several student resources such as scholarships, mentoring programs, career development webinars, and an annual conference. It is especially valuable for girls and young women exploring a future career in STEM fields.

Data Analyst

What Does a Data Analyst Do?

When professional basketball coaches want their players to score more baskets, they have to figure out the best way to make this happen. This is the kind of problem Ivana Seric was hired to solve. Her job was to analyze data on shooting and other aspects of the game for the Philadelphia 76ers professional basketball team. Among other things, her analysis would help the coaches determine which players shoot best in high-pressure moments. As a former college basketball player and someone who loves working with data, working in sports is a fulfilling path for her. "This is perfect," said Seric of the job. "There's math, there's basketball; it's a dream job for me."[10]

At a Glance

Number of Jobs
93,471 in 2023

Pay
Average pay $82,640 in 2025

Educational Requirements
Preferably a bachelor's degree in mathematics, data science, statistics, or similar

Personal Qualities
Discerning, innovative, communicative

Working Conditions
Typically, inside an office, at a desk

Future Job Outlook
Growth of 23 percent through 2033*

* Number is for operation research analysts, which include data analysts

Data analysts dig through large sets of data—numbers and facts. They look for patterns in the data. They offer their clients or employers insights into how those patterns can benefit their businesses or improve operations or better serve customers. Whether they work for private industry, government, nonprofit organizations, or other entities, their work helps inform decision-making. For example, data analysts might help the US Navy determine maintenance schedules for ships, help schools determine tutoring needs, or assist an ice-cream shop with determining its operating hours based on foot-traffic patterns in the neighborhood.

To accomplish their job, data analysts use software and programming tools to collect, organize, and analyze information. Once they have determined trends and developed their findings, they might create charts or presentations to communicate the information to those who sought it. When it comes down to it, their job is to understand what the data means and how it can be used to address the needs and concerns of clients or employers.

A Typical Workday

Radi Hilaneh is a health care data analyst at a biotechnology company that specializes in artificial intelligence–driven drug discovery and development. While his focus is on data, each day starts with a meeting. He and other analysts discuss their tasks for that day and brainstorm methods to complete them. For example, a task may be to review raw clinical trial datasets for errors, missing values, or inconsistencies to prepare it for analysis.

The rest of the day might be spent on the computer collecting, cleaning, and processing data. Medical databases make data collection fairly easy. Analysts like Hilaneh grab the data they need through queries using Structured Query Language (SQL) or other programming tools. This task can be quick if the databases are well organized and the request is straightforward. Next, Hilaneh cleans the data by removing errors or outliers—data points that differ significantly from other values—because they can skew results and create misleading patterns. Once the data is clean, he organizes it to make it easier to spot patterns and draw conclusions. He uses programming tools like Python and software like Jupyter Notebook designed for data analysis. These tools also let him display data in graphs or charts to better visualize patterns and trends. Hilaneh analyzes the graphs and charts of the differ-

A Bridge to Decisions

"As a Data Analyst, I've learned that the true power of data isn't just in collecting it, but in transforming it into insights that drive action. Whether it's identifying hidden trends, optimizing business performance, or predicting what's coming next—data analysis is the bridge between raw information and smart decisions. What I love most about this field? Every dataset is like a mystery to solve. Every dashboard is a canvas for storytelling. And every insight has the potential to spark real change."

—Yorqin Saipov, Excel analyst

Yorqin Saipov, LinkedIn, 2025. www.linkedin.com.

ent datasets to then provide information needed by his company. A typical project might involve using data from past clinical trials to forecast new trial outcomes or predict patient responses to treatments. His work helps the company make smarter, faster decisions in developing new medicines.

Hilaneh believes that his work has a positive impact on people, which makes the job feel especially rewarding. "My company analyzes DNA [deoxyribonucleic acid] related data in young people to predict future diseases such as Alzheimer's, Diabetes, Crohn's, and many more. This really changed my perspective on data analysis and made me feel like I'm making an actual difference in the world,"[11] explains Hilaneh.

Education and Training

Students interested in becoming data analysts can start preparing as early as high school. Taking computer science, statistics, or math classes is a great foundation for this career. Many high schools also offer courses in coding or data skills. Outside of school, students can explore free resources like Khan Academy or Codecademy to learn programming languages such as Python or R. Practicing how to sort data, filter it, and create graphs using tools like Microsoft Excel or Google Sheets builds valuable early skills.

Though some employers hire analysts who do not have college degrees but have completed technical certifications, most data analysts obtain a bachelor's degree in fields such as mathematics, statistics, business, economics, or computer science. In college they take courses in data analysis, statistics, and coding and learn to use professional tools like SQL, Excel, and Tableau. In addition to a college degree, many analysts also earn technical certifications to sharpen their skills and improve job prospects. Examples include the Google Data Analytics Certificate or Microsoft Certified: Data Analyst Associate. These credentials can help job seekers stand out—whether they are entering the field without a degree or adding to an existing one. For those who want to take their careers further, earning a graduate degree in data science or a related field can lead to leadership roles, such as managing teams of analysts or designing large-scale data projects.

Skills and Personality

A sense of curiosity is an important trait for a data analyst. Part of the job is looking at lots of data. An equally important part of the job is being curious about what the data shows. A data analyst's job is to try to understand why certain numbers are rising or falling or not moving at all. In some ways this is like solving a puzzle. Data analysts search for patterns among the many pieces of data in an effort to see and understand the bigger picture.

As challenges or questions arise, data analysts need to be both nimble and logical. And they need to be able to articulate their findings to people who might not be strong in analytics. Writing, speaking, and developing presentations with easy-to-understand visuals are important skills for interactions with executives, clients, and other decision-makers.

Technical skills are important too. Most analysts work with programs like Excel and SQL every day. They often use Python or R and tools like Tableau or Power BI to create dashboards and graphs and charts of data. Being comfortable with technology and able to learn as new technology emerges are key components of success in this career.

Workplace Settings

Analysts work in all types of industries and settings. They work in corporate offices, government agencies, hospitals, research firms, and tech companies. Some work in busy urban headquarters, while others are based in quieter suburban or regional offices. Many have flexible arrangements that include some form of remote work.

Data analytics can be a solitary job, or it can involve working with teams of people. This can depend on the size of the company or agency. Most analysts work a standard forty-hour week, with weekends and evenings off, making it a career that generally offers a good work–life balance. While extra hours may be needed to meet project deadlines, the flexibility and stability of the role make it appealing to many professionals.

Employers and Pay

Because data is used in nearly every field, data analysts work in a wide variety of industries. Even in fields that do not seem high-tech, data plays a role. School districts, local governments, and nonprofit organizations increasingly use data analysts to improve services and make decisions based on facts instead of guesswork. Some analysts work at large technology consulting companies that provide analysis for clients, while others work directly for an organization, so as to improve their services. Retail companies use analysts to study customer behavior, while sports organizations use them to scout talent or improve game strategy. Top employers include companies like Amazon, Google, JPMorganChase, and Meta, but there are also many roles at smaller firms, universities, start-ups, and nonprofits.

Salaries vary depending on experience, industry, and location. According to the online career search website ZipRecruiter, the average pay for data analysts was $82,640 as of May 2025. Entry-level data analysts may start with lower salaries, but those with advanced

Finding the Why

"Unlike many purely technical roles, a data analyst works closely with what's really happening in the company. Your insights directly influence decisions, sales strategies, and revenue. Why it's satisfying: You're not disconnected from reality—your analysis can drive real change. You learn how a business works—from marketing to sales to operations. Your work has meaning—you understand the 'why' behind every report."

—Kajo Rudziński, analytical data architect

Kajo Rudziński, "Why I Love Being a Data Analyst—4 Reasons to Choose This Career," Kajodata, April 8, 2025. https://kajodata.com.

skills in programming, statistics, or machine learning can earn significantly more. Analysts working in large cities or in high-demand industries like tech and finance often see higher pay as well.

Some data analysts go on to become data scientists, business intelligence analysts, or data engineers—roles that typically require more technical knowledge and bring higher pay. But even entry-level analysts often find the work rewarding and well compensated.

What Is the Future Outlook for Data Analysts?

For those who are interested in a career with long-term potential, data analytics is a smart choice. According to the market research and consulting firm Fortune Business Insights, the global data analytics market is projected to grow from $7.03 billion in 2023 to $303.4 billion by 2030. This growth is a result of the world producing more data than ever before—through smartphones, websites, streaming services, social media, medical records, and more. These changes are likely to increase the number of jobs in this field.

Companies want to use all that data to make better decisions. To do that, they need people who can find meaning in the numbers. As automation and artificial intelligence grow, data analysts will play an important role in helping humans and machines work together effectively. "Data analytics is the future, and the future is now!" says Hilaneh. "All the actions you do on your computer, smartphone or tablet are recorded and collected by a data analyst somewhere who is trying to make their business flourish. That's right—every mouse click, keyboard button press, swipe or tap is used to shape business decisions. Everything is about data these days. Data is information and information is power."[12]

Find Out More

American Statistical Association (ASA)

www.amstat.org

The ASA is a leading professional organization for statisticians and data scientists. It offers resources for students, including competitions like the Statistics Project Competition for grades 7–12, student chapters, scholarships, and mentoring programs. The ASA website provides access to educational materials, career resources, and opportunities to connect with professionals in the field.

Data Science Society

www.datasciencesociety.net

Data Science Society is a global online community that provides people with ways of building practical data science skills through challenges and collaboration with others. Its website offers online hackathons, data case competitions, and forums where students can learn from experienced analysts. It also provides link to data science current news.

Girls Who Code

https://girlswhocode.com

Girls Who Code is a nonprofit organization that focuses on encouraging girls to become involved in coding and information technology. Its programs include a vast array of topics, including data science. Its website offers free clubs for younger girls and teens, summer programs, and ways for college students to practice skills and find connections for internships and jobs.

Air Traffic Controller

What Does an Air Traffic Controller Do?

On February 23, 2025, at Phoenix Sky Harbor International Airport in Arizona, an air traffic controller spotted a potential crisis in the making. According to media reports, a Southwest Airlines plane and an American Airlines plane were both preparing to land. The Southwest crew had missed a radio instruction and was heading directly toward the other plane. The controller had only seconds to act and ordered the American Airlines plane to turn and climb. The pilot responded, and the planes narrowly missed each other. The controller had seen a problem and found a quick solution to avoid a tragedy.

Problem-solving, although not always this dramatic, is part of the job of air traffic controllers. They direct aircraft to ensure that millions of passengers safely reach their destinations. Using radar and other technology at airports large and small, controllers coordinate the movement of planes to maintain safe distances, manage the timing of takeoffs and landings, and keep air traffic flowing smoothly. To prevent collisions, they must make

At a Glance

Number of Jobs
More than fourteen thousand

Pay
Average salary of $144,580 in 2024

Educational Requirements
Associate's degree from Air Traffic Collegiate Training Initiative program preferred

Personal Qualities
Calm, precise, focused

Working Conditions
High-pressure situations, in tower or radar control room

Future Job Outlook
Growth of 3 percent through 2033

quick decisions in complex situations, such as sudden weather changes or unexpected aircraft maneuvers.

Although the job of all air traffic controllers is to keep the flying public safe, controllers have various specialized roles. Some controllers work in airport towers. Tower controllers rely on visual observations along with radar and electronic systems to direct air traffic once planes are within 3 to 5 miles (4.8 to 8 km) of the airport. They give pilots instructions for taxiing on the ground, taking off, and landing. Once a plane takes off, radar controllers typically take over. They usually work in the tower, but in specially equipped radar rooms. Working with radar sensors, the radar controller's job is to guide planes as they climb or descend, usually up to about 20 to 50 miles (32 to 80 km) around the airport and to an altitude of about 17,000 feet (5,182 m). Radar controllers keep planes safely spaced until the planes come under the guidance of the next group of controllers: the en route center controllers. En route controllers work away from airports, in big control centers across the country. They give pilots instructions, clearances, and updates on flight conditions, keeping thousands of planes moving safely on their routes.

For over a decade, Erin Domini has worked as an air traffic controller in New York Air Route Traffic Control Center. She always dreamed of becoming an air traffic controller, following in the footsteps of her mother. What she loves most is the constantly changing nature of the job and how meaningful the work feels. "The most rewarding part is just knowing that you're helping to keep these people safe. . . . I couldn't imagine doing anything else,"[13] says Domini.

A Typical Workday

The work of air traffic controllers is essentially the same whether they work in the United States or another country. One unnamed controller who works in Scotland says every day brings a new challenge. Some days he works in the radar room. In that capacity, he says, "I am the eyes of the airplane."[14] While working in the radar room, Airport Surveillance Radar and Air Route Surveillance Radar enable controllers to monitor aircraft position, speed, and altitude before they reach the airport. This allows them to give directions to pilots to keep the planes safely separated.

When working in the tower, controllers have their eyes on the planes. "You are making sure the airplanes are safe to land and take off, and that they have a stand [gate] to come and go from,"[15] the controller adds. Tower controllers mostly rely on visual contact with aircraft, but they also use radar. This provides extra help for managing takeoffs, landings, and ground traffic.

Complications often arise during controller shifts. Weather, mechanical issues, and airspace congestion require controllers to adapt constantly. "Theoretically, every plane should arrive at exactly the same time every day and then depart at exactly the same time every day. The fact is it just never happens like that,"[16] the controller explains.

Amid so much unpredictability, there is one constant. "You never forget that safety is the most important thing to us,"[17] he emphasizes. Making sure all planes and passengers reach their destination safely is the ultimate goal for controllers.

Education and Training

Because air traffic control involves spatial awareness, time and distance calculations, and understanding of how weather affects an aircraft, high school math and science courses offer good preparation for students who are interested in becoming air traffic controllers. Algebra, geometry, physics, and (if available) meteorology are all good places to start. Students should also take classes that strengthen communication skills. This is important because air traffic controllers must be able to communicate clearly with pilots in routine situations and when emergencies arise.

Never the Same

"Your hair is going to turn gray from the amount of stress. It's the most stressful job in the world. But . . . this job is fun. It's for people who don't like the mundane job of sitting in front of a desk, working 9 to 5 every single day. Every aircraft you handle is different. Every situation that you're going to handle is different. So while people try to deter you, I think for most of us . . . the challenge and even some of the stress makes it a little fun and it makes us enjoy our jobs."

—Haley Williamson, an Embry-Riddle Aeronautical University student majoring in air traffic management

Quoted in Mark Harper, "New FAA Initiative Offers 'Amazing Opportunity' for ERAU Air-Traffic Control Students," Yahoo!, April 24, 2025. www.yahoo.com.

In the United States, most prospective air traffic controllers obtain two-year or four-year college degrees from schools that are part of the Federal Aviation Administration (FAA) Air Traffic Collegiate Training Initiative program. These programs include courses in aviation basics, air traffic procedures, weather systems, and communication skills. Some prospective controllers combine other degrees with work experience or military experience.

No matter which educational route a person takes, all prospective air traffic controllers must apply to the FAA and, if accepted, attend the FAA Academy in Oklahoma City. To be eligible to work as an air traffic controller, candidates must be US citizens, be under age thirty-one at the time of application, and pass a medical and background check. To get into the academy, they also must achieve "well qualified" on the Air Traffic Skills Assessment test, which includes areas such as decision-making ability, spatial awareness, multitasking, and memory.

The FAA Academy course lasts for three to six months, depending on the job track. It includes intensive classroom and simulation-based training. From there, job candidates move to an assigned control tower or radar facility, where they undergo

Air traffic controllers direct flights in and out of airports and monitor aircraft along predetermined flight paths. Air traffic controllers must have strong problem-solving skills to deal with things like sudden changes in weather and unexpected aircraft maneuvers.

supervised on-the-job training. This stage can take two to four years to complete since some facilities are more complex and require more time for trainees to master local procedures and traffic patterns. Additionally, air traffic controllers continue receiving training and performance evaluations throughout their careers.

Skills and Personality

The job of an air traffic controller can be stressful—very stressful. Mental resilience in this field is a necessity. Often, controllers deal with issues outside of their control, adding to the pressure of knowing that lives are at stake. Jonathan Stewart is a veteran air traffic controller at the Philadelphia Terminal Radar Approach Control facility that handles flights headed to or from the Newark Liberty International airport. In 2025 FAA facilities that serve the Newark airport experienced staffing shortages and two blackouts, during which controllers lost their radar capability. During this time period, Stewart averted a midair collision between aircraft flying nose to nose. "I don't want to be responsible for killing

400 people,"[18] Stewart said when discussing the immense pressure he feels when dealing with these circumstances.

Controllers work with a lot of moving parts—on the ground and in the air. The job requires great focus and the ability to make precise decisions under swiftly changing conditions. Adaptability and a willingness to learn are also needed, since controllers must update their skills to keep pace with evolving technology and regulations.

Workplace Settings

Air traffic controllers work at airports of all sizes across the United States and around the world. At large US airports, they typically operate from tall, glass-walled control towers that overlook busy runways and taxiways, managing numerous commercial and cargo flights. In contrast, controllers at smaller airports often work in modest towers or rooms, overseeing fewer flights that may include commercial aviation, private aircraft, and student pilots.

The FAA has strict workplace rules for air traffic controllers. Because most airports operate twenty-four hours a day, seven days a week, air traffic controllers work rotating shifts to ensure continuous coverage. Controllers are not allowed to work more than ten hours per shift, including required breaks, and must have at least nine hours of rest between shifts. Many follow a rotating schedule called the 2-2-1 system—two afternoon shifts, two morning shifts, and one overnight shift each week. Ultimately, these rules are designed to protect controllers from fatigue, so they can stay sharp and keep people safe.

Employers and Pay

Nearly all air traffic controllers in the United States are employed by the FAA, which manages hiring, training, and certification for nearly all civilian controller positions. Controller jobs are available throughout the United States, but the highest concentrations of

A New Language

"Training for this job is challenging, because it's almost like learning a whole new language. You're talking in numbers and acronyms constantly, and getting everything to be able to pretty much say at a moment's notice is nerve wracking at times because of the huge responsibility that you have with each and every aircraft that's in the air. But it's fun, it's a lot of fun, but it is very challenging throughout the whole training process."

—Adam Guerrero, air traffic controller at Southern California Terminal RADAR Approach Control

Quoted in Mind on My Mission, "Air Traffic Contoller." https://mindonmymission.com.

jobs are typically found near major metropolitan airports and regional air traffic control centers. The pay is among the highest for careers that do not require a bachelor's degree, with the average close to $150,000 annually. Working for the FAA, a federal government agency, also comes with benefits such as a retirement plan, vacation days, and health and dental insurance.

What Is the Future Outlook for Air Traffic Controllers?

According to the Bureau of Labor Statistics, employment of air traffic controllers is expected to grow about 3 percent through 2033, which is about as fast as the average for all occupations. However, in 2025 the FAA announced a major shortage of controllers, despite more than eighteen hundred new hires in 2024. A fully staffed air traffic control system would require about three thousand more controllers. To solve the shortage, the FAA is actively recruiting. It has increased pay, enhanced benefits, and streamlined the hiring process.

The job is always challenging. Cedrick Earley, an FAA air traffic controller, shares his perspective. "I enjoy the challenge of coming in every day to a new puzzle," says Earley. "Controllers are always learning on the job, updating and refining processes or learning new rules and procedures. It's a job where you always have to change and adapt."[19]

Find Out More

Embry-Riddle Aeronautical University

https://erau.edu

Embry-Riddle Aeronautical University is a leading US academic institution focused on aviation, aerospace, and STEM education. Embry-Riddle offers degree programs tailored to aspiring air traffic controllers and aviation professionals. Its website includes details on courses, campus life, and industry partnerships that help students prepare for a career in the skies.

Federal Aviation Administration (FAA)

www.faa.gov

The FAA is the governing body of US airspace. Its website provides information on becoming an air traffic controller, including training requirements, application steps, and eligibility. The site also includes career development programs and hiring updates.

National Air Traffic Controllers Association

www.natca.org

The National Air Traffic Controllers Association is the union representing air traffic controllers. Its website explains what the job involves and the role controllers play to keep air travel safe. It includes descriptions of different types of controllers, the work environment, and the skills required to succeed in the field.

Electrician

What Does an Electrician Do?

In some houses and businesses, electrical wiring is predictable—lines follow a standard layout based on current building codes, and systems are modern. But that is not always the case, especially in older buildings and houses, where electrical systems can be outdated and barely up to code. That is when electricians become problem solvers, as they figure out how to repair or upgrade wiring with minimal disruption to the users of the facilities. "You are going to be presented with many different scenarios where it is going to be up to you to diagnose the problem, and figure out what's going on,"[20] says the "Mad Electrician," a licensed union electrician in Portland, Oregon, and popular YouTuber. Electricians ensure that lights turn on, appliances run smoothly, and critical systems—from heating and cooling to communication networks—function properly.

At a Glance

Number of Jobs
About 80,200 openings per year

Pay
Average salary of $62,350 in 2024

Educational Requirements
High school diploma and apprenticeship

Personal Qualities
Technologically adept, detail-oriented, flexible

Working Conditions
Indoor and outdoor at residential, commercial, utility, and construction sites

Future Job Outlook
Growth of 11 percent through 2033

On any given day, electricians might read and interpret blueprints, install wiring and circuit breakers, connect outlets and lighting fixtures, and test equipment for safety and code compliance. They use a variety of tools such as voltage testers, ammeters, pliers, and drills, and they follow both local and national electrical codes to keep people and property safe. When systems fail, electricians troubleshoot by drawing on their training and problem-solving skills to figure out what is wrong and how to fix it. Whether wiring a new house or upgrading an outdated electrical system, electricians play a crucial role in keeping modern life running.

A Typical Workday

A typical day for a residential electrician often begins early, starting with reviewing the day's scheduled clients and making sure all necessary tools and materials are ready. These might include hand tools like wire strippers, cutters, crimpers, and drills; testing devices such as voltage testers and multimeters; materials like wiring; and safety devices like circuit breakers.

The first job might involve diagnosing a nonworking outlet or figuring out the cause of a flickering light. After that, the electrician may head to another house to install a fast-acting circuit breaker outlet in a bathroom to meet safety codes. Some days involve several short appointments. Others might be spent entirely on one project, like installing a whole-house generator, which usually takes a full day and a whole team of people.

Troubleshooting is a regular part of the job. Electricians frequently inspect wiring, test electrical components, and track down the source of issues like recurring breaker trips or malfunctioning fixtures. Sometimes the work stretches into the evening or weekends, especially for emergency calls. Despite the long hours, the variety keeps the job engaging. Steve, a licensed electrician in Michigan, explains:

> It's hard to get bored in this career. One day you may be on top of a building, the next under a house. Here digging a trench by hand, there running conduit through an attic.

> One moment helping a client decide between LED or fluorescent lights—next fixing a broken conduit in the middle of a parking lot. Today climbing 50 feet up scaffolding, tomorrow under a sink installing power to a disposal.[21]

For commercial electricians, the day starts similarly—reviewing job orders and checking that all materials and tools are ready. These electricians work in places like office buildings, schools, hospitals, shopping centers, factories, and new construction sites. The morning might begin at a hospital to troubleshoot lighting issues or at a new warehouse to install electrical panels and conduit. On-site, they often consult blueprints to understand the electrical layout before starting. Tasks may include running wires through walls and ceilings, setting up control systems, or upgrading lighting and appliances to meet energy efficiency standards. Safety inspections and equipment testing are part of the daily routine, especially when dealing with older buildings that have outdated wiring.

New opportunities are also emerging in the field. Borin Reyes, owner of a small company based in Oakland, California, started by rewiring homes during renovations. His business has expanded through a partnership with another firm to install electric vehicle (EV) chargers for electric vehicles. As of 2023, they were installing about five EV chargers per week in addition to their regular residential work.

Education and Training

Becoming an electrician does not require a four-year college degree, but it does require special training, including lengthy hands-on work. Typically, the road to becoming an electrician starts with earning a high school diploma or general equivalency diploma. In high school, courses in algebra and physics help develop a strong foundation in problem-solving, measurements, and basic electrical

Apprentices Needed

"[The need for electricians] is a tremendous opportunity to get the word out about the union. We've always actively recruited in high schools, and now we're even in middle schools. Every chance we have, we're passing out flyers in neighborhoods and at job sites . . . especially in areas where we have a shortage of electricians."

—Adrian Sauceda, the International Brotherhood of Electrical Workers

Quoted in Bob Woods, "America's Demand for Skilled Electricians Is Entering a Boom Cycle," CNBC, July 27, 2024. www.cnbc.com.

concepts. Many high schools also offer career and technical education programs that include introductory electrical work, giving students hands-on experience with tools and safety procedures.

After high school, aspiring electricians normally enter a paid apprenticeship program. Applicants may be required to pass a basic aptitude exam that covers reading comprehension and ability to perform simple arithmetic and first-year algebra. Once accepted into a program, which lasts about four to five years, apprentices receive classroom instruction and on-the-job training with experienced electricians. Local unions like the International Brotherhood of Electrical Workers, nonunion contractors, and trade organizations all offer apprenticeship programs.

During training, apprentices learn how to install, maintain, and troubleshoot electrical systems. They also take classroom courses covering electrical theory, blueprint reading, the National Electrical Code, and safety practices. Anyone working as an apprentice, Steve recommends, should "assist and support your Supervisor in every way imaginable. This means whatever is needed at the moment. You will unload stuff in the morning and pack it back up at the end of the day. You will hand tools and materials to others. If someone needs anything, you are the guy/gal running to the truck to get it."[22] Doing so will show willingness to work hard, which will likely result in senior electricians giving the apprentice electrician more responsibility.

In most states, those who complete an apprenticeship have to take a licensing exam before they can work as an electrician. Licensing requirements can vary by state or region, but the exam typically covers knowledge of the National Electrical Code, electrical theory, safety procedures, and local laws and building codes. Before taking an exam, applicants are generally required to show proof that they have completed a specific number of hours in both classroom instruction and hands-on training.

Skills and Personality

Electricians need a mix of technical knowledge and strong decision-making skills to succeed on the job. Being self-motivated is essential, since many electricians make decisions on-site without direct supervision. Communication skills are also important for working directly with clients and with other tradespeople.

Being attentive to detail and alert to potential problems is important because safety is always the top priority. Working with electricity always carries risk, so safety is a critical part of the job. Live wires, high-voltage systems, and complex electrical components can cause serious injury or even death if handled improperly. Common injuries include getting shocked, being burned, and even falling if working on high-level wires. Fatal injuries are also possible due to high-voltage shocks. That is why electricians must strictly follow safety procedures and regulations. As Borin Reyes, owner of Boyes Electric, puts it, "You really have to be focused, because of safety. You have to be hands-on most of the time and solving problems. That's one of the things that I like best—solving problems."[23] This mindset—staying alert, thinking critically, and understanding the technical aspects of the work—helps electricians perform their job safely and effectively day after day.

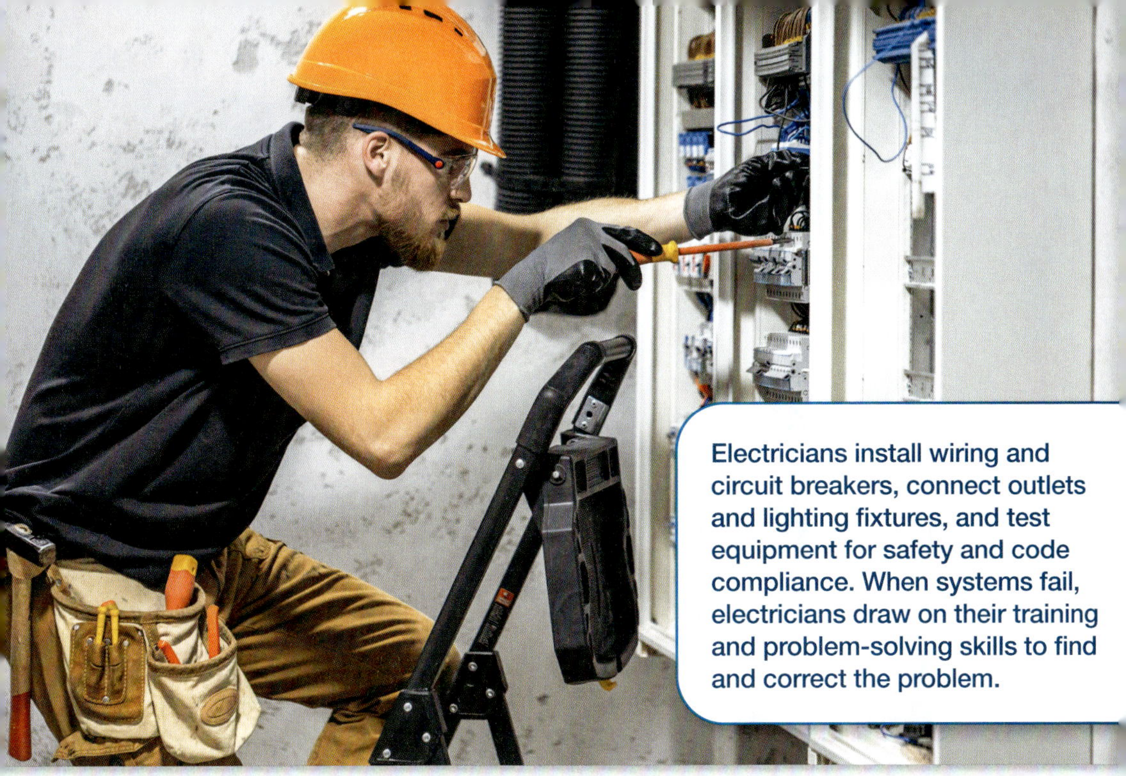

Electricians install wiring and circuit breakers, connect outlets and lighting fixtures, and test equipment for safety and code compliance. When systems fail, electricians draw on their training and problem-solving skills to find and correct the problem.

Workplace Settings

Electricians may spend part of the day in the office working on scheduling, payments, and planning for upcoming jobs, but most of their work is on-site—in houses or apartments, commercial buildings, or construction sites. Those working in their own company or with a smaller company often operate independently and must solve problems on their own. In contrast, commercial or industrial electricians typically work as part of a team with architects, engineers, and other construction professionals on larger-scale construction projects. Their work can be indoors or outdoors, depending on what the job entails. While work can be on a regular schedule, overtime, including weekends or evenings, is not uncommon.

Employers and Pay

Most electricians are employed by companies that are hired to work for residential or commercial clients (or both). Electricians might also work for government agencies, construction companies, or utility companies, or they might be self-employed. Apprentice electricians

Hands-On Puzzles

"I really like solving problems and working with puzzles. I don't mind getting dirty. I'm a fix-it kind of person; it's kind of my personality. I love the feeling of having something broken and then fixing it. I like working on cars and fixing stuff."

—Karen Huff, veteran electrician

Quoted in Suzanne Wisler, "Lambertville Woman One of Country's Few Female Electricians," Yahoo! News, January 16, 2024. www.yahoo.com.

earn about 40 percent of what journeymen electricians make. Pay increases once they complete their apprenticeships. According to the Bureau of Labor Statistics (BLS), the average annual wage for electricians was $62,350 in May 2024, but electricians can make over $100,000 depending on their experience, location, and company. As Steve explains, "Not only does the electrician enjoy steady and satisfying work, the electrician's salary and wages are the highest paid of the skilled trades due to the technical knowledge and diverse skills that are required to perform a broad range of tasks."[24]

What Is the Future Outlook for Electricians?

Nearly every building depends on electricity, so electricians are always in demand to install, upgrade, or replace these systems. As newer energy sources like solar panels and wind turbines become more popular, this should lead to even more opportunities for electricians. As these systems are added to homes and businesses, skilled electricians will be needed to connect these systems to local power grids. Also, BLS data shows that about 21 percent of electricians will hit retirement age in the next ten years. For these reasons, the BLS estimates an 11 percent rise in demand for electricians through 2033, which is much higher than the average.

Find Out More

Independent Electrical Contractors (IEC)

https://ieci.org/apprenticeship

IEC offers a paid apprenticeship program that combines classroom learning with real-world job experience and is offered throughout the United States. Its programs are approved by the US Department of Labor. On its website, there are details about how to apply, where to train, and what to expect from the program.

International Brotherhood of Electrical Workers (IBEW)

https://ibew.org

The IBEW offers hands-on apprenticeship programs through the Electrical Training Alliance. Its website includes details about training opportunities, application steps, and local union contacts to get started.

National Electrical Contractors Association (NECA)

www.necanet.org

The NECA offers apprenticeship programs in partnership with the International Brotherhood of Electrical Workers. In addition to information on apprentice programs, its website provides information about a variety of electrician-related topics, such as safety codes, wages, and more.

Cybersecurity Analyst

What Does a Cybersecurity Analyst Do?

A hospital's entire computer system shuts down. Doctors cannot access patient records, and surgeries are delayed. Cybercriminals have used malicious software (called ransomware) to lock the files on a computer or network. Someone needs to figure out how it happened and stop it from happening again. For those who like solving high-stakes puzzles and using technology to protect people and systems from incidents like this, cybersecurity might be the right path to follow. "A sharp analytical mind and strong problem-solving skills are the greatest assets a cybersecurity analyst can possess,"[25] writes Frank Jones, a Java coder and cybersecurity researcher. Cybersecurity analysts defend the networks and computer systems used in virtually all organizations, from schools and hospitals to banks, government agencies, and the military. They keep hackers out and make sure important data stays safe.

> ### At a Glance
>
> **Number of Jobs**
> About 17,300 new openings annually
>
> **Pay**
> Average salary in 2025, $82,554
>
> **Educational Requirements**
> Preferably a bachelor's degree in cybersecurity or related field
>
> **Personal Qualities**
> Composed, inquisitive, comfortable with technology
>
> **Working Conditions**
> In an office; possible shift work and overtime
>
> **Future Job Outlook**
> Growth of 33 percent through 2033

Cybersecurity analysts respond to threats and set up defenses to protect computer systems. They observe their screens for unusual activity in their logs keeping watch across the network. Sometimes they work alone, especially in smaller companies, while larger organizations have full security teams of people who collaborate to monitor and protect massive computer systems.

In addition to monitoring for breaches and responding to incidents, cybersecurity analysts have a variety of other responsibilities. Their daily tasks might include scanning systems for vulnerabilities, installing and managing firewalls and encryption software, and conducting regular risk assessments and penetration tests (a simulated and planned cyberattack on the organization's computer system, network, or application) to find weaknesses before actual attackers do.

Analysts also investigate suspicious activities such as unusual log-ons or unauthorized devices connecting to the network, draft detailed incident reports, and work with other departments to educate employees about implementing cybersecurity best practices. They use digital tools like intrusion detection systems, encryption programs, and threat intelligence reports to stay a step ahead of cyberattacks.

A Typical Workday

A typical day for a cybersecurity analyst often starts with checking emails and attending meetings with managers or other analysts, where they may discuss new protocols to implement, recent cyber threats, planned testing, or ongoing security projects. Following this, many analysts spend the day scanning the network for any potential issues. "My workday typically involves me logging into my organization's security information and event management system to hunt through volumes of alerts from various endpoints [devices such as computers, laptops, mobile phones, and servers accessing the network] and detection sources scattered across our organization,"[26] explains Anthony Messina, a cybersecurity analyst with a company that develops software to monitor, detect, investigate, and respond to cyber threats.

Messina reviews alerts to determine whether there is suspicious activity on the network, such as a strange log-on from a country the company does not work with regularly. In this case he would dig deeper and look to see whether the login is a threat or just an employee working remotely. To check, he determines factors like the user's location, device, and time of access, and he verifies with the employee, if available, on whether they accessed the system remotely.

If the log-on poses a threat, a cyber analyst must work quickly to protect the system. This may include blocking harmful internet protocol addresses, updating the firewall (a security system that controls incoming and outgoing network traffic), and patching vulnerabilities to shut things down before any damage is done. Messina explains that actual threats provide extra challenges, but they also keep the work interesting. "Occasionally those juicy malicious indicators of compromise will land in my dashboard, and I will get to work alongside our incident response team to begin scoping out the true damage that specific alert behavior or file caused,"[27] Messina explains. The mix of routine monitoring and unexpected incidents keeps the job interesting and intellectually stimulating.

Education and Training

Information technology classes like computer science, cybersecurity, or Advanced Placement Computer Science Principles can help high school students build a solid foundation in programming, problem-solving, and understanding cybersecurity basics. Outside of school, students who are interested in becoming cybersecurity analysts can start learning to use the tools commonly used in the field. For example, with free online tools and trial versions, they can get familiar with vulnerability management software, antivirus programs, and password manager programs.

Growing Market

"The global cybersecurity market size is estimated to reach 281 billion by 2027, and that is a lot of cybersecurity jobs that are going to need good cybersecurity professionals to fill them, and with more of the world coming online, building applications, having websites . . . they're going to need a lot more cybersecurity professionals."

—Sandra, cybersecurity analyst

With Sandra, *What Does a Cybersecurity Analyst Do: How to Become a Cyber Security Analyst? Salary, Skills, Roadmap*, YouTube, September 4, 2022. www.youtube.com/watch?v=r90Fp_DycDU.

Many future cybersecurity analysts earn four-year college degrees in cybersecurity, computer science, information technology, or a related field. But that is not the only path to a career as a cybersecurity analyst. Some people start with an associate's degree and gain experience or earn certifications. Popular certifications for anyone in this field include CompTIA Security+, CompTIA Cybersecurity Analyst, and Certified Ethical Hacker. Those who enter this field should plan on keeping up with changes in technology and with constantly evolving scams.

Skills and Personality

Having a strong interest in technology—and the ability to understand how it works—is essential for anyone wanting to become a cybersecurity analyst. Most of the job involves working with specialized software tools, monitoring network activity, and analyzing online data to detect and prevent threats. A natural curiosity about how systems work is important to stay up-to-date in this fast-changing field.

People who are fast learners, organized thinkers, and able to stay focused during stressful situations are more likely to succeed in the job of a cybersecurity analyst than people who do not have

The Best People

"The folks in this industry understand the impact of what they are doing. And the impact of what happens if they don't do it well. It is full of some of the most hardworking, committed people who are fighting an uphill battle every single day. So if the mission and the impact don't get you, the people will."

—Sara Goodison, cybersecurity professional

Sara Goodison, "Six Things I Love About Working in Cyber Security," Medium, January 10, 2020. https://medium.com.

these traits. Ryne Sherman is chief science officer with a global firm that handles personality assessment tools for business hiring. Sherman believes that technological skills and aptitude matter but maybe not as much as personality when it comes to the job of a cybersecurity analyst. "While these [skills] are important, it is crucial to remember that personality traits play a huge role. A candidate with the suitable personality can be easily trained into the right role,"[28] says Sherman. For example, one of the most important traits for a cybersecurity analyst is the ability to quickly learn new information. New types of cyber threats emerge every day, and analysts have to stay up-to-date on what those threats are and how to defend against them. Another key trait is staying calm under pressure. When a security incident happens, analysts must remain composed as they quickly assess the situation and decide how to respond to protect the organization's network and data. In a field that is constantly changing and critical to protecting organizations' systems, having the right mindset can be just as valuable as having the right skills.

Workplace Settings

Most days cybersecurity analysts work on their computers in office environments. They might take part in meetings, either in person or online. They might also work with employees to make sure they are aware of cyber threats and how to avoid them. The job is often fast-paced and intellectually challenging, requiring constant analysis, quick decision-making, and ongoing learning. While many analysts work regular weekday hours, the nature of cybersecurity means that emergencies can arise at any time. If a threat occurs, overtime or after-hours work may be necessary, and some roles—especially in government or military settings—may involve rotating shifts to provide around-the-clock coverage.

Employers and Pay

Cybersecurity analysts are in high demand across all types of companies and organizations—from tech start-ups and financial institutions to hospitals, schools, and retail businesses. Keeping data and computer systems safe from hackers, viruses, and unauthorized access is a top priority in nearly every industry. Federal agencies such as the US Department of Homeland Security and the Federal Bureau of Investigation have traditionally relied on cybersecurity analysts to defend against cyberterrorism and espionage. State and local governments also employ analysts to help protect public infrastructure, schools, and sensitive data systems.

The cybersecurity field is a high-paying one due to the high level of technical knowledge and the importance of the work. According to Payscale, an online platform that provides salary data and career resources, average salary for a cybersecurity analyst in 2025 was $82,554. Salaries differ based on years of experience. According to Payscale, entry-level analysts earned $70,828; analysts with five to nine years of experience earned $94,380; and analysts with ten to nineteen years of experience earned $109,124.

What Is the Future Outlook for Cybersecurity Analysts?

Cybersecurity is one of the fastest-growing fields in the United States, and the demand for skilled analysts keeps rising. As technology expands into every area of life, more industries are hiring cybersecurity professionals to protect computer systems and sensitive data. The education sector is increasingly bringing on analysts with the need to secure student records and e-learning platforms. The automotive industry is another growing area, especially as more vehicles become connected and autonomous. The energy sector, too, needs cybersecurity experts to protect power grids and other vital infrastructure.

Cybersecurity analysts are increasingly needed in order to stay ahead of complex, constantly changing threats. "As 2025 unfolds, the cybersecurity landscape continues to evolve at a breakneck pace, shaped by groundbreaking technologies, shifting regulations, and increasingly sophisticated threats. Key areas such as cryptographic advancements, third-party risk management, and AI-driven threats demand immediate attention from organizations across industries,"[29] writes Steve Lasky, editorial director of the Endeavor Business Media Security Group. With so many expanding opportunities and high demand, the outlook for cybersecurity analysts is strong and expected to keep growing.

Find Out More

Cyber Magazine

https://cybermagazine.com

Cyber Magazine is a leading digital publication focused on cybersecurity. It covers topics such as network, application, operational, and cloud security. It provides the latest news about cybersecurity, including threats and leaders in the field around the world.

Cybersecurity and Infrastructure Security Agency (CISA)

www.cisa.gov

The CISA, part of the US Department of Homeland Security, leads the US effort to understand, manage, and reduce risk to the nation's cyber and physical infrastructure. Its website offers free cybersecurity services and tools, including links to both its own and third-party software like vulnerability scanners, intrusion detection systems, and endpoint protection.

National Cybersecurity Alliance (NCA)

www.staysafeonline.org

The NCA is a nonprofit organization dedicated to making a more secure digital world. Its website offers free resources such as articles and videos, training, and events focused on educating people about cybersecurity best practices, data privacy, and online safety.

Source Notes

Introduction: A Way of Thinking

1. Akanksha Chapra, "About," LinkedIn. www.linkedin.com.
2. Quoted in Morgan McFall-Johnsen, "A Teen Won $12,500 for Building a Playground out of Recycled Tires. She Plans to Build 3 More Parks Across Nigeria," MSN, April 11, 2025. www.msn.com.

Forensic Scientist

3. Quoted in Rhianna Benson, "Forensic Expert Reveals the One Mistake Serial Killers Make That Always Gets Them Caught," Tyla, May 28, 2024. www.tyla.com.
4. Quoted in Erin Kent, "Interview with George Schiro, Forensic Scientist, Scales Biological Laboratory," eLearners. www.elearners.com.

Environmental Engineer

5. Quoted in Careersnz, *Environmental Engineer*, YouTube, 2023. www.youtube.com/watch?v=yr9Vi8w3k54.
6. Quoted in *Ferrovial* (blog), "Hannah Olonovich, from Webber, Shares Her Thoughts in This Interview About International Women in Engineering Day," June 23, 2020. https://blog.ferrovial.com.
7. Quoted in *Ferrovial* (blog), "Hannah Olonovich, from Webber, Shares Her Thoughts in This Interview About International Women in Engineering Day."
8. Quoted in *Ferrovial* (blog), "Hannah Olonovich, from Webber, Shares Her Thoughts in This Interview About International Women in Engineering Day."
9. Randy Ly, *Why You Need to Work as an Environmental Engineer*, YouTube, 2024. www.youtube.com/watch?v=B9ardXgCq8U&t=413s.

Data Analyst

10. Quoted in Shydale James, "A Whole New Ball Game: Alumna Scores Job as Data Scientist for Philadelphia 76ers," NJIT. https://news.njit.edu.
11. Quoted in Tom Taylor, "A Day in the Life of a Data Analyst—What's It Really Like?," Career Foundry, June 22, 2023. https://careerfoundry.com.
12. Quoted in Taylor, "A Day in the Life of a Data Analyst—What's It Really Like?"

Air Traffic Controller

13. Quoted in Federal Aviation Administration, *Meet an Air Traffic Controller: Erin Domini—New York Center*, YouTube, 2020. www.youtube.com/watch?v=dRwkL2uRGW8.
14. Quoted in Air Navigation Solutions, *A Day in the Life of an Air Traffic Control Officer*, YouTube, 2021. www.youtube.com/watch?v=9H-VWC6eSsQ.
15. Quoted in Air Navigation Solutions, *A Day in the Life of an Air Traffic Control Officer*.
16. Quoted in Air Navigation Solutions, *A Day in the Life of an Air Traffic Control Officer*.
17. Quoted in Air Navigation Solutions, *A Day in the Life of an Air Traffic Control Officer*.
18. Quoted in Amanda Musa, "Veteran Air-Traffic Controller Speaks Out About Staffing and Tech Problems amid Black-outs and Delays at Newark Airport," CNN, May, 16, 2025. www.cnn.com.
19. Quoted in Taylor Rains, "AA Plans to 'Supercharge' Air Traffic Control with Faster Hiring and Pay Raises. What You Should Know Before Applying to the High-Stress Job," MSN, 2025. www.msn.com.

Electrician

20. Mad Electrician, *20 Reasons Why I Love Being an Electrician*, YouTube, 2021. www.youtube.com/watch?v=oFya3AHOvCw.

21. Steve, "How to Become an Electrician: Complete 5-Step Guide," Ask the Electrical Guy, 2024. https://asktheelectricalguy.com.
22. Steve, "How I Survived My First Year as an Electrician Apprentice," Ask the Electrical Guy, 2024. https://asktheelectricalguy.com.
23. Quoted in Emily Pontecorvo, "To Ditch Fossil Fuels, We'll Need to Raise an Army of Electricians," AfroLA, May 16, 2023. https://afrolanews.org.
24. Steve, "How to Become an Electrician."

Cybersecurity Analyst

25. Frank Jones, "Cyber Security Analyst Job Description," Cyber Experts, October 23, 2023. https://cyberexperts.com.
26. Quoted in Liz Simmons, "A Day in the Life of a Security Analyst," Cyber Degrees, December 8, 2022. www.cyberdegrees.org.
27. Quoted in Simmons, "A Day in the Life of a Security Analyst."
28. Quoted in Hogan, "The 8 Personality Traits to Succeed in Cybersecurity," May 2, 2023. www.hoganassessments.com.
29. Steve Lasky, "Cybersecurity 2025: Preparing for an Evolving Threat Landscape," Security Info Watch, January 6, 2025. www.securityinfowatch.com.

Interview with a Cybersecurity Analyst

Matthew Lemma is a chief information officer and chief information security officer (CISO) with CI Azumano Travel, a travel management organization. He answered questions about his career by a phone interview.

Q: Why did you become a cybersecurity analyst?

A: When I was coming up in the IT [information technology] field, I was often assigned tasks related to information security—before it really became its own specialized field. I found that I enjoyed that kind of work. What pulled me in the most was being the person who helps an organization understand how to protect its information and implement countermeasures to defend against cyberattackers. As part of my current role, I lead both offensive and defensive cybersecurity strategies. It's rewarding because, at the end of the day, I know I've made an impact in keeping our systems and data safe.

Q: Can you describe your typical workday?

A: We are a service organization, and our company's goal is to ensure availability, confidentiality, and integrity for our clients. My daily work ties directly into that mission by protecting their information. On a typical day, we handle user issues related to software or other technical problems. We also work on engineering projects—fixing anything that's broken in the network or making improvements to prevent future problems. For example, if a server is getting too old to function properly or can't be updated anymore, we may decide to replace it. Another major part of the job is incident management—responding to security issues. I personally spend a lot of time in this area, overseeing potential threats. This means identifying the threat, determining the source, reviewing logs to understand what happened and when, and then taking steps to mitigate the issue. Sometimes it's as simple as changing a password; other times, it's much more complex. Training is also part of the day. A good CISO guides the organization with continuous education on cybersecurity. I personally train every new person who joins the team to make sure they understand how to stay safe and protect our systems.

Q: What do you like most about your job?
A: What I like most is knowing that I'm doing something good—for both the company and its customers—by protecting them. I develop and implement strategies to defend against threats from our nation's adversaries. It's not just about safeguarding company and customer data—we also help protect government information. Hackers often try to reach government systems by targeting private companies like ours that work with the government. I also enjoy that this work requires thinking ahead—always anticipating future threats and figuring out how to prevent them before they happen.

Q: What do you like least about your job?
A: What's challenging is that you're the one who gets the call if anything related to information security goes wrong. There's no room for an off day—you always have to be ready to respond to any incident or issue. It's a high-pressure, high-risk job, and one mistake can lead to serious security consequences.

Q: What personal qualities do you find most valuable for this type of work?
A: Definitely the ability to learn and be adaptive. There's a lot of continual learning in this field. You also need to have an engineering mindset for finding solutions. And being cool and level-

headed is essential—you're often faced with new situations and potential threats that require immediate action.

Q: What advice do you have for students who might be interested in this career?

A: When I interview people just out of college, I'll ask if they can tell me about their home routers. If they're into gaming, I might ask if they know the specs of their computer or gaming systems. Questions like that help me see whether they're genuinely curious about the technology they use. So, for teens, I'd say—start by asking *why*. Why do things work the way they do? How is your own data being secured? That kind of curiosity is important.

Other Jobs If You Like Problem-Solving

Artificial intelligence specialist
Bioinformatics technician
Biomedical engineer
Chemical engineer
Civil engineer
Computer systems analyst
Construction manager
Crime scene technician
Database administrator
Data engineer
Data scientist
Detective
Electrical engineer
Epidemiologist
Ethical hacker
Fire protection engineer
Geographic information system (GIS) analyst
Hydrologist
Industrial engineer
Intelligence analyst
Logistics coordinator
Network administrator
Operations research analyst
Penetration tester
Plumber
Private investigator
Quality assurance specialist
Robotics technician
Software tester
Water resource specialist
Wind turbine technician

Editor's note: The online *Occupational Outlook Handbook* of the US Department of Labor's Bureau of Labor Statistics is an excellent source of information on jobs in hundreds of career fields, including many of those listed here. The *Occupational Outlook Handbook* may be accessed online at www.bls.gov/ooh.

Index

Picture Credits

Cover: Metamorworks/Shutterstock

10: ZUMA Press Inc/Alamy Stock Photo
19: goodluz/Shutterstock
34: Gorodenkoff/Shutterstock
43: PV productions/Shutterstock

About the Author

Leanne Currie-McGhee has written books for the past two decades. She lives in Norfolk, Virginia, with her husband Keith, daughters Grace and Sol, and their dog Delilah.